Data Strategy Canvas for Healthcare Organizations

Table of Contents

The Big Picture	1
Getting Started	7
Creating Your Canvas	9
Next Steps	19
Sample Canvas	21
About the Author	25

The Big Picture

The opportunities for realizing your mission through the use of data multiply by the day. Healthcare organizations now have access to an astonishing array of digital assets that would have been unthinkable even 10 years ago. Indeed, the future of healthcare organizations will increasingly rely on their ability to creatively use data that powers new programs, services, products, and initiatives.

With that said, this massive variety of data creates a challenge: how can you create a comprehensive data strategy with so many options to choose from? In my work with healthcare organizations to develop data-driven programs, I am often asked:

- Where do we start?
- How do we choose what to focus on?

- What do we do next?

Many of the traditional tools for strategic planning are not well-suited for creating a fluid, adaptable data strategy, and complex planning processes can leave your team disengaged and confused. It is for these reasons that Breakthrough Healthcare created the Data Strategy Canvas.

If you're looking for a treatise on management science and strategic planning, this is not the book for you. That terrain has been well mapped by others, and I am assuming that you're already familiar with much of it. My goal is instead to help you move quickly from planning to solution development, rather than spending time on analysis and re-analysis before taking action.

The Data Strategy Canvas will guide your team through rapidly capturing the key internal and external factors influencing your opportunities with data, and how to synthesize this information into actionable, mission-oriented solutions. After your team develops its Canvas, you'll have a clear path to developing mission-oriented programs and products using a variety of data sources.

Mission: Only a data strategy aligned with mission can realize across-the-board value.

Program areas: What are the big-picture strategic goals of your program areas, and how could using data change the way you achieve them?

Data assets: Which data assets are aligned with your strategic program goals? Which assets are feasible to use and attainable?

Programs & services: What new offerings and benefits can you create from data assets, and how can you improve your existing offerings?

Stakeholder ecosystem: Who is aligned with your mission? Who provides benefits to your members, and who do they provide benefit to? Who wants to leverage your expertise, trust, and reach to achieve mutual goals?

Mission:

Goals

Landscape

Partners:

Competitors:

Stakeholders

Opportunities:

Threats:

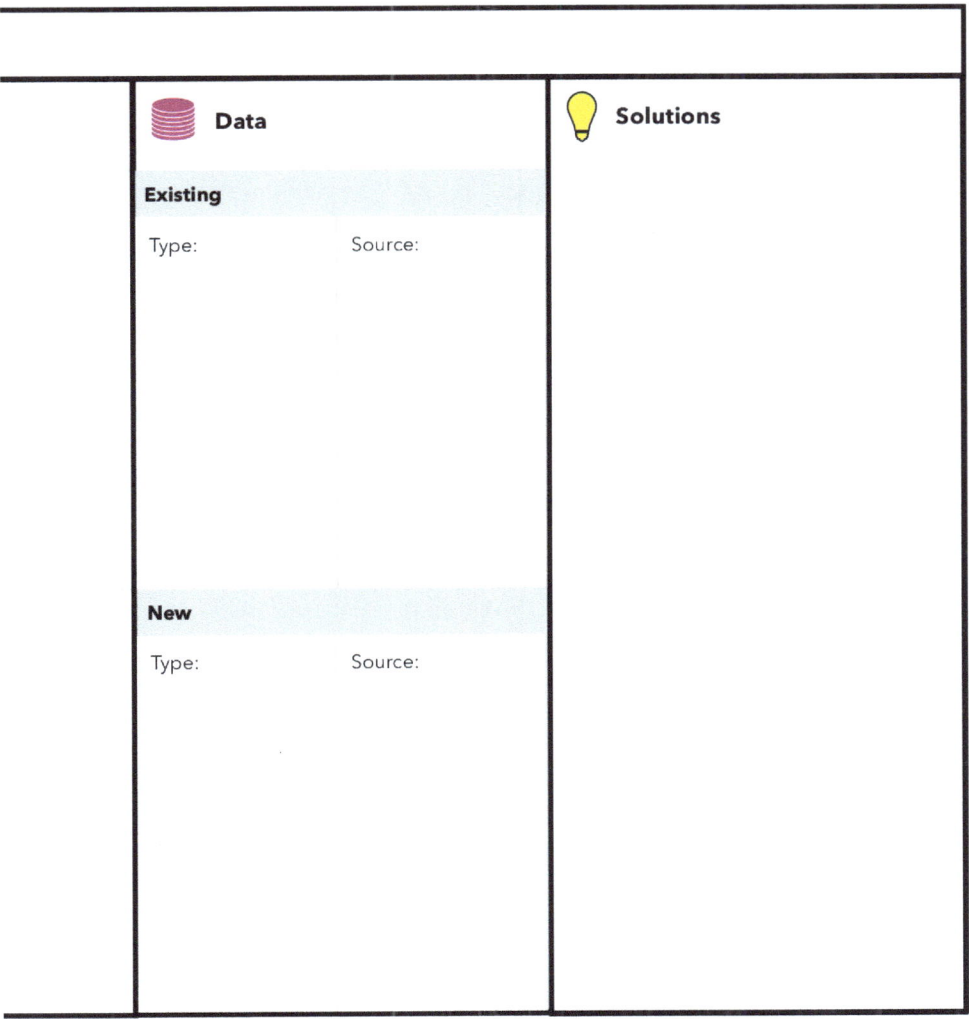

Getting Started

Data strategy design is a team sport, requiring the input of a broad spectrum of organizational stakeholders. We recommend the following format to quickly and effectively complete your Data Strategy Canvas:

Bring the Team Together

You will be working closely and building your Canvas in real-time, and as such, this activity is by far most effective in-person. Your team should include leaders from across your major programs and priority areas.

Plan to Spend a Day

Schedules are always tight, but the creation of a holistic data strategy is worth a full day of your team's time. Make sure that team members provide their undivided attention to the exercise; checking email and taking calls signals that a team member is disengaged from the process.

Find a Big Whiteboard

You're going to be generating a lot of ideas, priorities, and resources - make sure you have plenty of room! Completing each section of the Canvas with sticky notes gives you the flexibility to rearrange, reword, and add new ideas.

Work Left to Right, Top to Bottom

After filling in your mission at the top, work your way through each section of the Canvas, from Goals, Stakeholders, Landscape, Data, and finally, Solutions.

Discuss and Reflect

Your team will accomplish a tremendous amount in the course of the day, and providing time for everyone to reflect and discuss will help to further refine your Canvas.

Creating Your Canvas

The Data Strategy Canvas is designed to quickly surface your organization's priorities, data opportunities, and innovative ideas that will serve as the foundation for your data strategy. In this section, we'll walk through each part of the canvas, how to complete them, and how the part different parts of the Canvas interact with one another.

Mission

Your organization's mission statement is the first part of the Canvas, and is prominently located at the top. When exploring opportunities with data, it can be easy to develop great ideas that creep outside of your mission. We put mission first and foremost on the Canvas to ensure that your ideas remain in your organization's wheelhouse, and are focused on meeting your stakeholders' needs.

As you design your Canvas, return to your mission frequently, asking yourself and others if each part of the canvas is truly mission-focused. If the answer is no, it's time to reevaluate that part of the Canvas and make adjustments to remain on-mission.

Goals

The Canvas is built from left to right, starting with the Goals you identify for your organization. Your Goals may already be defined in your strategic plan, or you may develop a set of goals specific to using data to meet member needs.

Strategic goals are often organized by department or practice area. If your existing goals are broken down this way, begin by reframing to make them organization-wide. An effective data strategy breaks down departmental barriers and uses data to the benefit of the entire organization and its stakeholders.

Stakeholders

The healthcare ecosystem is comprised of a vast array of interconnected stakeholders. In membership organizations like medical societies and associations, the member is always the primary stakeholder. However, by considering an expansive network of stakeholders in developing your data strategy, you will realize new opportunities that would not otherwise be possible.

When developing your stakeholders section, consider the following:

- Who are your direct stakeholders, such as members and customers?
- Who are your indirect stakeholders, such as employers, purchasers, regulators, standards-setting bodies, and affiliated or allied healthcare entities or specialties?
- Cross-reference with your goals: Are there stakeholders that could benefit from your goals, but are not on the Canvas?

Landscape

Landscape scans are a key component of all strategic planning, and your data strategy is no different. The Data Strategy Canvas expedites landscape scanning, focusing on the four components that will most impact your strategy.

Partners

Data-driven initiatives can be costly and complex. Working with partners and collaborators is a way to share costs, gain access to experienced human capital, spread risks, and meet the needs of a broader group of stakeholders.

When developing your partner section, consider the following:

- Include not only partners and collaborators that you have already worked with, but also potential partners and collaborators.
- Who do you partner or collaborate with most frequently, and why?
- Who do you not partner with that serves one or more of your stakeholders, and why?

- Who are unlikely or unexpected partners that you haven't considered?
- Cross-reference with your stakeholders: What potential partners or collaborators meet your stakeholders' needs, but aren't on your partner list?

Competitors

In contrast to the opportunities presented partners, competitors represent threats to meeting your stakeholders' needs and achieving your goals. Moving too quickly into a space with existing or likely competitors can be extremely risky, in terms of costs, reputation, and diversion of resources.

When developing your competitors section, consider the following:

- Who do you compete with directly on strategic initiatives?
- Who do you compete with indirectly on strategic initiatives?
- Who serves your stakeholders and could become a new competitor?
- What non-organizational competitors exist? For example, a competing option to participating in one of your regulatory reporting programs could be to choose not to participate in any regulatory reporting at all and pay penalties instead.
- Cross-reference with your goals and partners: What competitors share the same goals, and what would it take to convert them to allies?

> **Unnecessary competition creates risk!**
>
> All organizations have competitors and "frenemies." When developing your data strategy, consider:
>
> - What are the potential risks to your organization if it competes and loses?
> - Is it to the benefit of your stakeholders for you to compete, or would it be to their benefit if you collaborate instead?
> - Are there unmet stakeholder needs you can address instead of directly competing with others to meet the same needs?

Opportunities

In this part of the Canvas, you'll really start pulling together the other pieces that you've already completed. The opportunities you identify should be based on the goals you've established, stakeholders you work with, potential partners or collaborators, and potential competition.

When building your opportunities, keep the following in mind:

- Don't restrict yourself to opportunities that may seem immediately achievable. This is a good time to think creatively and expansively about all of the opportunities that are available, no matter how audacious they may seem.
- Are there opportunities that you have declined before, but are still viable now?
- What do opportunities do you see when when you look through the eyes of each of your stakeholders?
- What opportunities are available to your partners and competitors?

Threats

Threats are the environmental factors that can hinder your progress toward achieving your goals. Similar to Opportunities above, your Threats section should be based on your established goals, stakeholders, partners, and competitors.

When building your Threats section, consider the following:

- What threats are real at this time? What theoretical threats do you face?
- What evolving threats are small now, but have the potential to grow in the future?
- What threats do your partners and competitors face? Are they the same threats as yours?
- What threats do you your stakeholders face?
- What are the threats of inaction?
- Cross-reference with your goals and opportunities: How can one or more of your threats be converted into opportunities?

Dude, where's my SWOT?

You probably recognize Opportunities and Threats as parts of the Strengths, Weaknesses, Opportunities, and Threats (SWOT) framework. SWOTs have been used for decades to classify and organize the findings of environmental scans.

We happen to think that the SWOT analysis is past its prime. After all, Strengths present Opportunities, and Weaknesses create Threats. We recommend focusing on known and emerging opportunities, and how to mitigate threats or convert them into new opportunities. It's a much simpler, actionable approach compared to a complex SWOT matrix.

Data

Up until now, you may have been wondering why your Data Strategy Canvas hasn't involved "data" yet. The reason is that the question of "what data should we use" has an endless number of answers if it isn't first refined by a set of goals, environmental opportunities, and challenges.

With your goals, stakeholders, and landscape as a guide, think about the types of data that could be used to create solutions to meet your needs. The data do not be closely defined at this point; the most important part of this process is to create an inventory of relevant data and data sources that could be used to meet your goals.

Existing Data

Begin with data that you already have available to your organization. Your organization probably has a variety of data already, such as website usage information, learning management system records, membership management system data, and clinical registry data. While no single data source will meet all of your needs, each holds important pieces that can be combined to create innovative solutions.

New Data

After capturing your current data, think about the new types of data that could meet your goals. It is not important to consider feasibility or availability at this phase; instead, build a "wishlist" of data types and the sources you could get them from.

When building your list of new data, consider the following:

- The data you want may not exist in a single place. You may need to combine two or more sources of data to meet your needs.

- Similar data may be available from multiple sources. List all of the sources you know, and plan to evaluate those sources when you're considering business cases for your ideas.

- It's possible that some data may be completely new, and would require you or another organization to begin collecting it for the first time.

- It is possible that some of the data could be captured through a change to your existing systems, such as adding a field to your membership profile, adding a new question to your annual survey, or adding a clinical data element to your registry.

Solutions

You're now ready to begin the creative and analytical process of combining everything you've captured into potential programs, products, services, or initiatives. During this phase of completing your Canvas, you'll synthesize what you've learned to create ideas for achieving your goals through data.

As you craft solutions, be sure to refer frequently to the other parts of the Canvas. It is very likely that during solution development you will identify new stakeholders, partners, competitors, opportunities, threats, and data. Update the Canvas as this happens, and reflect on how each change impacts the Canvas in its entirety.

As you draft solutions, consider the following:

- Don't limit yourself to the most pragmatic or short-term ideas—this is the perfect time to think big!
- As you create a solution, refer to your data sources and consider how you can blend data to achieve something more valuable than if you use only a single type of data.
- Look across your goals and then cross-reference with your data lists to determine where you may be able to achieve multiple goals at once through a single data-driven solution.
- As you create solutions, return to your stakeholders list—are you meeting all stakeholders' needs, or do you need new or refined solutions to do so?
- Do your solutions take advantage of all of the opportunities you identified? Do they address all of the threats?
- Where can you leverage partners to create solutions that you can't develop on your own?
- What solutions have your competitors created, and how can you learn from their experience to develop something better?
- Are your solutions the same as those from competitors? What would it mean to compete?

Next Steps

The process of developing your Data Strategy Canvas will give you and your team a plethora of goal-focused ideas that will form the core of your data strategy. After finishing your initial Canvas, it's important to take time to reflect on your work, and consider where refinements or additions can be made. Take pictures of your Canvas, and convert it into a digital document for distribution to the team as soon as possible after the meeting, while everyone's memory is still fresh.

Rank Your Solutions

Your team should make any additional refinements, and then proceed to ranking solutions in order of priority. You can use any method you like for doing this, as long as feedback is incorporated from the entire team. After picking your top solutions and finalizing the Canvas, it can be helpful to print the Canvas on a poster and put it in a prominent place where team members can view it and leave comments.

Evaluate Business Cases

Develop a business case for each of your top solutions focusing on the feasibility, financing, market demand, and competitive landscape for the solution. If a viable business case cannot be found for a particular solution, you can move on to the other solutions that you developed when creating your Canvas. When viable business cases are determined for a solution, it is time to proceed with planning and development for that solution.

Reflect and Refine

As you formalize your strategy through your selected solutions, it is important to continue to meet regularly with your data strategy team to review progress, and determine if there are new factors that should be reflected in your Canvas. The Data Strategy Canvas is meant to be organic, and adapting and growing over time as you realize new opportunities and choose new goals.

Sample Canvas

# Pinky Toe Pain Physicians Association

 Mission: Improve the lives of pinky toe pain (PTP) patients through physician education,

Goals

Increase physician use of PTP education programs

Improve responsiveness to regulatory changes affecting PTP practice

Provide quality measurement tools and drive improvement in the treatment of PTP

Develop a research network for PTP

Landscape

Partners:

Toe Pain Society

Hangnail Quality Coalition

Health insurers

Pinky Toe Quality Alliance

Competitors:

Society for Pinky Toe Professionals (SPTP)

MyPinkyToe.com

Shady Open Access Journal of Toe Medicine

Opportunities:

New foot quality program incentives from Payor X

Recent guideline update

Merger of PinkyToeMed & ToePro EHRs

Threats:

New SPTP quality registry in development

Changing quality measures

PTP reimbursement cuts

 ## Stakeholders

Physician members

PTP patients

PTP physician employers

Health Insurers

American Board of Toe Medicine (ABTM)

research, and quality improvement.

Data		💡 Solutions
Existing		Analyze web usage, education usage, and quality measure data to identify new education program topics.
Type:	Source:	
Clinical	PTP Registry	
Physician list	CMS NPI	Modify PTP Registry measures to include new payor and CMS measures, and incorporate CMS cost data, linked by NPI, to argue for incentives and prevent reimbursement cuts.
Education Use	LMS	
Interest areas	Website	
New		Partner with Hangnail Quality Coalition and Pinky Toe Quality Alliance to use PTP Registry and hospital discharge data to create Pinky Toe Quality Accreditation Program.
Type:	Source:	
Cost	CMS PUFs	
New quality measures	Updated PTP Registry	
LOS, Dx, Px, charges	Hospital discharge data	Link PTP Registry and SPTP Registry to build new research network.

About the Author

Sam Walters, MBA, CAE

Sam is the founder and President of Breakthrough Healthcare. In his 20-year career, he has worked across diverse healthcare organizations in the domains of clinical registries, quality measurement and improvement, research, technology, clinical guidelines, marketing, and organizational strategy. He has worked as both an employee and consultant to over 25 healthcare organizations, including medical societies, healthcare technology and analytics providers, accreditation organizations, health systems, government agencies, and patient advocacy foundations. His diverse skillset includes strategic and business planning, market research, patient registry and clinical dataset design, quality measure design, quality improvement program design, digital product development, research program development, data analytics, corporate relations, and business process improvement.

Breakthrough Healthcare

Breakthrough Healthcare is a consulting firm that provides clinical program design, organizational strategy, and product development services. Our clients include nonprofit medical societies, healthcare membership associations, government agencies, and data-driven healthcare enterprises.

Our mission is to create healthcare solutions that transform challenges into opportunities, leverage the experience of those we serve, develop the expertise of our clients, and exceed all expectations for success.

Contact Us

8120 Main Street, Suite B
Ellicott City, MD 21043 USA
+1 (443) 266-8015
hello@breakthrough.healthcare
http://breakthrough.healthcare

Copyright © 2019 Breakthrough Healthcare

All rights reserved. No part of this book may be reproduced in any form or by any electronic or mechanical means, including information storage and retrieval systems, without permission in writing from the publisher, except by reviewers, who may quote brief passages in a review.

www.ingramcontent.com/pod-product-compliance
Lightning Source LLC
Chambersburg PA
CBHW040301220526
45473CB00002B/551